Bathtub Science

**SHAR LEVINE &
LESLIE JOHNSTONE**

Illustrations by Dave Garbot
Photography by Jeff Connery

Sterling Publishing Co., Inc.
New York

To all my girlfriends, who keep me sane: Leslie, Vicki, Maryann, Lorrie, Pauline, Lynn, Cinnamon, Lesley, and especially Shira—S.L.

To Shar and Vicki, for bringing so much fun into my life—L.J.

Acknowledgments

We are more grateful than words can express to Michael Bull and his wonderful staff at Cantu Bathrooms in Vancouver, B.C., for the use of their showroom, fixtures, tchotchkes, and overall amazing hospitality. Without them, this book wouldn't have been possible. Thanks also to Jeff Connery for his wonderful photography, Dave Garbot for his great illustrations, and to all of our extremely well-behaved and patient models: Chris, Nick, Megan, Alan, Emily, Jessica, Monica de Lazzari, Lauren Chan, Bianca Chan, Aaron Chan, Robin Anna Phipps, Alan Phipps, Evan Puri, and Derek Puri.

Library of Congress Cataloging-in-Publication Data Available

1 3 5 7 9 10 8 6 4 2

Published in paperback in 2006 by Sterling Publishing Company, Inc.
387 Park Avenue South, New York, N.Y. 10016
© 2000 by Shar Levine and Leslie Johnstone
Distributed in Canada by Sterling Publishing
℅ Canadian Manda Group, 165 Dufferin Street
Toronto, Ontario, Canada M6K 3H6
Distributed in the United Kingdom by GMC Distribution Services
Castle Place, 166 High Street, Lewes, East Sussex, England BN7 1XU
Distributed in Australia by Capricorn Link (Australia) Pty Ltd.
P.O. Box 704, Windsor, NSW 2756, Australia
Printed in China

Sterling ISBN-13: 978-0-8069-7185-8 Hardcover
ISBN-10: 0-8069-7185-1

ISBN-13: 978-1-4027-4094-7 Paperback
ISBN-10: 1-4027-4094-8

For information about custom editions, special sales, premium and corporate purchases, please contact Sterling Special Sales Department at 800-805-5489 or specialsales@sterlingpub.com.

Contents

Introduction

You think of your bathtub as a place to get clean, but did you also know that your bathtub can be an amazing science laboratory? You can learn all sorts of interesting scientific facts about water, what it's made up of, and how it works—and all sorts of other surprising scientific stuff—while you are scrubbing off dirt and grime.

Or you can do the experiments in this book when you're not taking a bath. Just put on some play clothes or wear an old smock as a "lab" coat, gather up your materials, and use the bathtub as a science lab while you stay nice and dry.

In fact, since not everyone has a bathtub at home, we've made sure that all of the ex-

periments and activities in this book can also be done in a bathroom or kitchen sink, or even in a plastic tub or a little wading pool in the backyard. However you decide to do them, always make sure you have your mom, dad, or teacher with you to help you complete all the steps of the experiments safely and explain anything you might not completely understand. The wonderful part is, even if you need some help to learn these new facts and ideas about science, once you've learned them you'll be able to explain loads of new things to all your friends. And you'll have lots of fun while you're learning—

you'll get to see how a submarine works, create a tiny tidal wave, watch flowers bloom in the water, and blow lots of beautiful bubbles!

You're about to become a mad bathtub scientist. So get ready for lots of adventures right in your own house, grab a towel, and let's get started!

Fun Bathtub Fact

Almost four thousand years ago, a Greek ruler named King Minos eased himself into a nice, hot bath after a long, hard day of ... well, being king! But his bathroom was hardly old-fashioned. It had both hot and cold water, a fountain decorated with gold, silver, and jewels, and even a toilet that flushed! There is no mention in the history books that he performed science experiments while getting clean, but his was one of the earliest bathtubs.

NOTE TO PARENTS AND TEACHERS

We all know that children learn best when they're enjoying themselves, so this book is designed to give you and your younger kids a way to start discovering some basic scientific principles by completing activities and experiments that are lots of fun. We all know, too, that it can be quite a challenge to get kids in the bath at home, and the activities in this book provide a great way to make bath time fun. All of the experiments in this book can be done while a child is at home taking a bath while supervised by his or her parents, or "tub-side" supervised, too. But you don't need a bathtub to teach your child or student the lessons about science that you'll find in this book. If you live in an apartment or house without a bathtub, or if you are doing these experiments with your students at school, you can turn a kitchen or classroom sink into a "laboratory," use a large plastic tub or foil pan, or fill a kiddie pool outside and do the experiments outside on a warm summer day.

All of the experiments in this book are exciting and safe for kids, but whenever a small child is in or around water, adult supervision is a must. Many of the experiments in this book require an adult helper, and we

strongly recommend that you be present for those few that don't actually require that you help with the steps themselves. Be very careful with water **temperatures**, do not let your child come in contact with any kind of soap or solution that might bother sensitive skin, and remove any potentially harmful objects or products from your child's reach. If you choose to share the activities in this book with your child or pupil, be sure to take the time to make sure that the environment in which you're working is in all ways a safe learning environment.

"Bathtub" science is safe, clean, fun, but it can get messy. It's mostly only water, after all, but have some towels on hand for small, unexpected spills. That said, get ready for your little ones to get a whole new attitude about bath times, turn on the taps, and prepare to learn some fun science with your kids!

SAFETY FIRST!

Safety is important no matter what you're doing or where you are, so if you are ever unsure about whether it's safe to do something, ask an adult. Your adult supervisor—whether it's your parents or teacher—will be able to guide you safely through the experiments in this book. Meanwhile, here are some definite "do's" and "don'ts" to get you started.

Do's

1. Make sure an adult is with you to supervise you while you do these experiments.

If you are doing this experiment in the tub, make sure an adult runs the bath for you and tests the temperature before you get in. He or she must make sure the water in the bath is not too deep. Use a rubber mat on the bottom of the tub to prevent you from slipping or sliding.

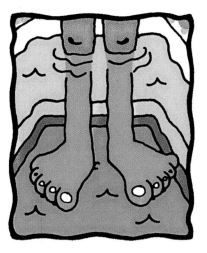

2. Tell an adult immediately if you hurt yourself in any way.
3. Read all of the instructions for an experiment before you begin any of the steps.
4. Keep a washcloth handy, in case you get anything in your eyes.

5. If you have sensitive skin or allergies, make sure your parent or teacher decides which experiments you do.

6. Have fun! And pick up all your equipment and materials when you are finished with an experiment, and put them away.

3. Don't use anything with batteries or anything that's electric in or near the water.

4. Don't eat, drink, or taste any of the materials used in the experiments.

5. Don't touch water in any form that's too cold or too hot.

Don'ts

1. Don't take a bath without adult supervision.

2. If you are doing experiments in the bathtub, don't take anything sharp or breakable in with you.

MATERIALS

- aluminum foil
- apple
- astringent
- baby oil
- baby shampoo
- balloon
- bath mat
- bowl
- bubble bath

- can opener
- coins
- colored paper

- cookie sheet or plastic tray
- cornstarch
- cotton balls
- cups (paper, plastic, and Styrofoam)
- dishwashing liquid
- double-sided tape

- dried fruits and vegetables
- duct or electrical tape
- Epsom salts
- eyedropper
- fishing weights
- food coloring
- funnel
- hammer
- hot-glue gun
- ice cubes
- jar with lid
- ketchup packets
- lids
- masking tape
- measuring cup
- measuring spoons
- milk carton
- modeling clay

- ○ nails
- ○ pens
- ○ plastic bowls
- ○ plastic containers (clear)
- ○ plastic figurine
- ○ plastic fruit basket
- ○ plastic pop bottles

- ○ plastic wrap
- ○ recorder or whistle
- ○ rubber bands
- ○ ruler
- ○ scissors
- ○ shaving cream
- ○ soap
- ○ sponges
- ○ straws
- ○ string
- ○ sugar
- ○ thimble

- ○ tin cans
- ○ tissue paper
- ○ toothpicks
- ○ towels
- ○ toys
- ○ tray
- ○ tubing, plastic and rubber
- ○ turkey baster
- ○ washcloth
- ○ watch (with second hand)
- ○ wire mesh
- ○ wooden skewer

Fun Bathtub Fact

You may have received letters and cards in the mail, and probably even a pretty big package or two—a birthday present, maybe, or a gift for another holiday. Or maybe you or your parents have ordered clothing, toys, or something for the house from a catalog. But can you imagine something as big as a bathtub coming in the mail? It's hard to picture in your mind, but it's true!—in the 1800s in the United States, a person could order bathtubs, sinks, and toilets through the mail.

Go, Rubber Ducky!

Do you have a rubber ducky that takes a bath with you? We bet you do. Everyone likes rubber ducks—even grown-ups! In Vancouver, Canada, there is a rubber ducky race each year. Thousands of ducks, each wearing a racing number, are released upstream in a river. The person whose duck crosses the finish line first wins! But here's the real question: Why do these ducks, and your own rubber ducky, float, while other toys sink? Let's find out.

WHAT YOU NEED

- apple
- bathtub
- metal spoon
- pencil
- plastic utensil or ruler
- rubber ducky
- sponge
- toys (safe and suitable for use in the tub)
- water

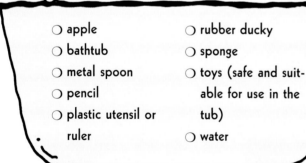

WHAT YOU DO

1. Place one object in the bath. Does it **float** or sink?

2. Do this again, this time with another object. What happens this time?

3. Place all the objects that floated in one group and all the objects that didn't float in another group. What do the objects in each group seem to have in common with the rest of the objects in their group?

4. Take each of the objects that floated and gently push them under the surface of the water. Hold each one there for a few seconds. Do they still float?

WHAT HAPPENED?

Some of the objects floated and others did not. Whether an object floats or not depends on a number of things. An object that is hollow and filled with air will stay afloat (like your rubber ducky did). So will an object whose size and shape make it spread out a little over the water's surface.

Solid objects float or sink because of something called **density**.

A small, heavy object such as a metal spoon, for example, has more density than the water, and so it sinks. A lighter object, such as a pencil, has less density than the water and so it floats. Some materials sink after being pushed into the water because they fill up with water and become heavier.

Crazy Thermometer

When you think of a drinking straw, you probably only think of it as something through which you sip your favorite juice or soft drink. Take another look, though—it's the same basic shape as a thermometer like your mom or dad uses to take your temperature when you're sick, right? Do you think you can take someone's temperature with a straw? Not really. But let's see if you can turn a straw into something that can measure temperature.

WHAT YOU NEED

- adult helper
- bowl
- food coloring
- hammer
- ice cubes
- jar with lid (small, the size of a baby-food container)
- modeling clay
- nail
- straws (several, all clear, in different widths)
- water

WHAT YOU DO

1. Have an adult hammer a hole into the center of the top of the jar. The hole must be wide enough so that individual straws of different widths can fit through it.

2. Fill the jar about ¾ full with water, add a couple of drops of food coloring, and tightly screw the lid on the jar. Insert one of the straws in the hole. Fix the straw in place by using modeling clay to seal the area around the straw where it meets the lid.

3. Hold the jar upright and slowly lower it into a bath or bowl filled with warm water until it is halfway submerged. Watch the level of the colored water inside the straw rise.

4. Take the jar out of the water and hold it in your hands to warm the water inside it. What happens to the liquid inside the straw? Does it go up or down?

5. Fill a bowl with cold water and ice cubes (if you used a bowl, rather than the tub, for step 3, empty the bowl first!). Lower the jar into the cold water so that most of it is submerged. What happens to the colored liquid inside the straw now?

6. Remove the first straw and repeat steps 1 through 5 using a wider straw. How far does the water level inside the straw rise this time? What do you think would happen to the level of colored water inside the straw if you used a super-thin straw?

WHAT HAPPENED?

When you placed the jar into the warm water or warmed it with your hands, the colored water inside the straw rose. When water is warmed up, it **expands** or swells up. When you place the jar into ice water, the water contracts, or shrinks, and moves back down the straw. Because the jar is sealed, the water has nowhere to go except up inside the straw. The same amount of water rises higher in a thin straw than a thicker one. **Thermometers** work in much the same way. They have a fat area at the bottom full of liquid and a very thin tube that acts like your straw—the hotter you are, the higher the liquid rises!

N(ice) and Easy

Do you like to swim? If you've ever tried floating in the ocean or a swimming pool, you know that when you take a deep breath, your lungs fill up with air and you are suspended in the water. Ice cubes also float, but not because they are filled with air—and they certainly haven't taken swimming lessons! You know that ice is made of water. So why does an ice cube rise to the water's surface? Let's take a look.

WHAT YOU NEED

- ○ ice cubes
- ○ measuring cup (large)
- ○ 3 plastic bowls or containers (shallow, all the same size)
- ○ 3 plastic cups (all the same size)
- ○ water

WHAT YOU DO

1. Fill one glass to the top with ice cubes. Fill the second glass with ice, then add enough water so that the glass is filled to the top. Fill the third glass to the brim with water.

2. Arrange the three bowls or containers on a tray or along the side of the tub, and place one of the filled plastic cups upright in each of them.

3. Let the filled glasses sit awhile, and watch the ice melt. In which glass does the ice melt first?

5. When the ice has melted completely, pour the water from each bowl and glass into a measuring cup. Which cup holds the most water? Which holds the least?

WHAT HAPPENED?

The ice by itself in a glass melted first, because the air is warmer than the water. Water

gets bigger, or has more **volume**, when it is frozen; when it thaws, or turns to liquid again, it has less volume, or gets smaller. The first cup holds the least water, and the third cup holds the most water. An ice cube floats because it weighs less than the amount of water that would take up the same space.

The Soup Cracker Mystery

You may have eaten a kind of soup called clam chowder, which comes with a little packet of crackers that you put in the soup. Ever noticed what happens to the crackers when you plop them in the soup? Something funny—they start out crisp, floating on the surface of the soup, but soon they become soggy and sink to the bottom. What is it that makes them turn to mush and disappear from sight?

WHAT YOU NEED

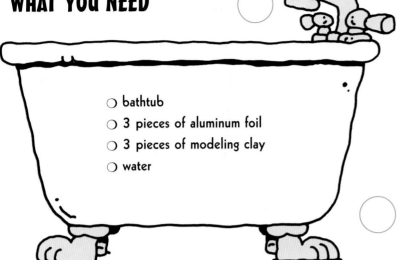

- ○ bathtub
- ○ 3 pieces of aluminum foil
- ○ 3 pieces of modeling clay
- ○ water

WHAT YOU DO

1. Roll one piece of clay into a simple ball shape. Place the second piece of clay against the rim of the tub or a counter and use your hand to flatten the clay out until it is thin and wide. Roll the third piece of clay into a ball, then stick your thumbs inside the ball and use your fingers to shape the ball into a boat. If you have any trouble, ask an adult for help shaping the clay.

2. Place each of the pieces of clay into the bathwater. Which shapes float and which shapes sink?

3. Try this again, this time using aluminum foil. Roll one piece of foil into a ball. Flatten out a second piece of foil. Fold up

the edges of a third piece of foil to form a boat shape. Which of the aluminum shapes float? Which ones sink?

WHAT HAPPENED?

Even though clay and foil seem like very different kinds of materials, the clay ball acted like the aluminum-foil ball, the flat piece of clay acted like the flat piece of aluminum foil, and

the clay boat acted like the boat made from aluminum foil. The boats and flat pieces hold in air in much the same way that dry crackers hold air inside them when they are first put into soup. They are more spread out over the water's surface, and more water is holding them up, so they float longer. When materials are squished into small balls, they have less air inside and less water holding them up, so they sink faster, like the clay and aluminum foil balls did. After crackers have been sitting in soup for a while, they begin to lose the air inside them and sink. Next time you have lunch with a friend and put crackers in your soup, you can explain the mystery!

Anchors Aweigh!

If you get out of the bath and step on a scale when you are still dripping wet, the number on the scale will be higher than when you weigh yourself when you are dry. Any idea how much more you might weigh if you weighed yourself while you were still soaking wet in the bath, with your whole body submerged? Well, you certainly can't put a scale into the bath! But there is a way you can weigh something in the bath. Huh? Here's a fun way to find out how.

WHAT YOU NEED

- adult helper
- bathtub
- piece of string approximately 12 inches (30 cm) long
- ruler or piece of wooden dowel
- 2 fishing weights (medium-sized and identical)
- 2 pieces of string, each approximately 1 yard (1 meter) long
- water

WHAT YOU DO

1. Have an adult help you tie and secure one end of a long piece of string around the top of one of the weights so that equal amounts of string are free on each side of the weight.
2. Using the second piece of long string and remaining fishing weight, repeat step 1.
3. Tie the remaining short piece of string to the middle of the ruler and hold the other end up. Have an adult help tie the free ends of strings attached to each weight to the ends of the ruler, so that one weight hangs from each end. He or she will need to adjust the strung weights so that when you hold the ruler up by the middle string, the weights hang at the same level. This is your "scale."
4. Stand beside the tub and have your adult helper balance the weights with one end hanging just above the water level and the other outside of the bathtub. Slowly lower the string so that the weight on the inside of the tub is surrounded by water. What happens to the other weight?

WHAT HAPPENED?

When you hold the scale so that neither weight is in the water, it is balanced. When one of the weights is placed into the water, the other weight drops downwards. The fishing weight doesn't weigh as much when it is submerged in the water as it did in the air. This makes the weight in the water lighter than the weight in the air, so the ruler tilts. Even though it doesn't seem as though the submerged fishing weight is floating, the water is holding it up.

Pop Bottle Hip-Hop

There's a rumor that some kids have been told by their parents that they must clean up their rooms because they are too messy. There's a scientific principle called **entropy** that helps explain this problem. Entropy means that "everything tends to become less organized and less orderly over time." The next time your parents ask you why your room is always so messy, you can tell them it has nothing to do with how tidy you are—it's all because of entropy! Of course, there's a very good chance that this won't change their minds about whether you have to clean up the mess or not. This next activity will show you how entropy works and also do something that seems like magic—it will teach your money how to dance!

WHAT YOU NEED

○ adult helper
○ bathtub
○ coins
○ plastic pop bottle
○ refrigerator
○ water

WHAT YOU DO

1. Place a coin over the top of the bottle. Choose the coin that fits best over the bottle's opening and most tightly seals the bottle. Keep this coin handy for the experiment.

2. Have your adult helper place the empty bottle in the fridge for about an hour, so it is really cold. (You don't need to put the bottle in the freezer.)
3. Have an adult hand you the cold bottle.

4. Dip your hand in water and add a few drops of water to the rim of the bottle. Place the coin on the wet rim. The water will form a seal between the coin and the rim of the bottle.
5. Hold the bottle in two hands and slowly lower it into warm

WHAT HAPPENED?

The water warmed the air in the bottle. When air is warmed up, its entropy increases and the molecules (tiny particles) that make up the air move faster and away from each other, to become more disordered. This made the air expand, or swell up. When the air

water. Make sure you keep the bottle level, so the coin doesn't fall off. Your coin should start dancing. If it doesn't, check the seal to make sure there is water between the coin and the rim of the bottle.

in the bottle swelled up enough, it pushed up on the coin and  some of the air escaped. The coin dropped back down and sealed the mouth of the bottle again. Then the air began to swell up some more, and each time the coin lifted and dropped back down, more of the air escaped.

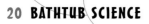

Playing Ketchup

Ever notice that when you get food from a fast-food or Chinese restaurant, you often wind up with enough packets of ketchup or soy sauce to put on King Kong's cheeseburger or fried rice? Well, apart from helping out the Earth by making sure you only take the number you need, you can put extras you don't use on your own burger or fried rice to use in a nifty science experiment. If you can't imagine how a simple packet of ketchup can let you make a scientific discovery, just wait—you're about to find out!

WHAT YOU NEED

- bathtub
- plastic bowl
- packets of ketchup or soy sauce (several plastic or foil, small and rectangular)
- 2-quart (2-l) clear plastic pop bottle with lid
- water

WHAT YOU DO

1. Fill the bowl with water and place unopened packets of soy sauce or ketchup in a bowl of water. Find a packet that just floats in the water, that doesn't float exactly on the surface of the water but doesn't sink to the bottom of the bowl.

2. Fill the clear plastic pop bottle with water, but leave several inches of air space at the top. Push the fast-food packet into the pop bottle. (You may need to fold it a little to get it through the opening.)

3. Put the lid on the pop bottle so that the bottle is tightly sealed.

4. Squeeze the sides of the bottle and watch what happens to the packet. Now try putting the whole bottle into a tub filled with warm water. What happens to the packet inside the bottle now?

WHAT HAPPENED?

You made something called a "Cartesian Diver." The food packet contains a small amount of air. When you squeezed the sides of the bottle, you compressed the air in the packet and the packet sank. When you let go of the sides of the bottle, the air inside the packet expanded and the packet rose. It is harder to make this happen in the warm water because the air inside the packet expands more in warm water than in cooler water.

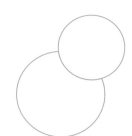

Submarine Fun

If you've ever visited a tropical place, you may have gone underwater in a special kind of submarine that allows the people riding inside to see fabulous sea creatures—all kinds of bright and unusual-looking fish and plants and other things—without getting wet. If you haven't taken a ride in a submarine, you've probably read about one, or seen one on television, or learned about submarines in a class or on the Internet. But how does a submarine actually work? Here's a simple way to understand.

WHAT YOU NEED

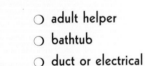

- adult helper
- bathtub
- duct or electrical tape
- hot-glue gun
- modeling clay
- plastic pop bottle with lid (large)
- plastic tubing
- 3 fishing weights (very small)

WHAT YOU DO

1. Have your adult helper use the hot-glue gun to melt three holes approximately 1 inch (2.5 cm) apart along one side of the plastic bottle. Have the adult use the glue gun to melt a hole in the center of the lid of the bottle just big enough for the tubing to fit through.

2. Place each fishing weight lengthwise next to one of the holes, and use a small piece of the tape to attach the weights to the bottle.

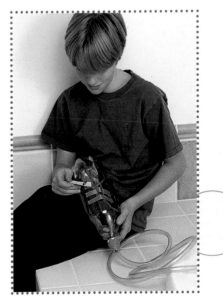

3. Thread one end of the plastic tubing through the hole in the lid so that approximately 2 inches (5 cm) of the tubing extends inside the bottle. Then, making sure that the tubing stays in the position you've just put it in, use a little bit of modeling clay to seal the area between the lid and the tubing. This is your "submarine."
4. Put your submarine into the bathwater. Push the submarine to the bottom of the tub so that it fills completely with water.
5. Blow through the plastic tubing and watch what happens to the sub.

WHAT HAPPENED?

When you pushed the bottle under water, it filled up with water and sank to the bottom. The side of the bottle with the holes and fishing weights was heavier, so this side faced down toward the bottom of the tub. As you blew into the plastic tubing, the air from your breath began to fill up the bottle. When enough air was inside the bottle to make it

float, it began to move upward in the tub. Finally, air began to come out of the holes on the bottom side of the bottle, and bubbles started to rise.

Wave Hello

Near the island of Oahu in Hawaii, there's a part of the ocean called the Banzai Pipeline, where surfers ride waves that are almost as big as a house! It's fun to ride small waves in the ocean when you visit the beach, or even just to stand and feel them around your ankles. But there's a way to study waves close up without even going outdoors. Can you guess how? Nope, we don't mean by watching them on TV—all you need are a few simple things you can probably find in the kitchen. Let's take a look!

WHAT YOU NEED

- baby oil
- bathtub
- food coloring (blue)
- plastic bowl
- plastic jar (small and clear) with lid
- water

WHAT YOU DO

1. Do this step in the kitchen over a sink (our sink has a funny bird-faucet to keep an eye on things, but you can use a regular sink, too!). Fill the jar about halfway with water. Add several drops of food coloring to the water so that it turns a nice blue shade.

2. Fill the rest of the jar with baby oil, then tightly screw the lid on the bottle. This is your wave **machine.**

3. Turn the jar sideways and slowly move your hands up and down. Watch the blue water inside the bottle. What's it doing?

4. Now, try a wipe out! Shake the jar up and down and watch the water and oil. What happens now?

5. Next, dip the bowl in bathwater and fill it up to the top. Try to move the bowl from one side of the tub to the other, without spilling any of the water in the tub. What happens to the surface of the water as you move the bowl? Why can't you stop the wave inside the bowl?

WHAT HAPPENED?

You made your very own Banzai Pipeline! When you added oil to the water in the jar, the two things did not mix. But when you shook the jar, the two liquids moved to-

gether but didn't mix together all the way. When you stopped moving the jar, the liquids separated again. There is a scientific  idea that says, "like dissolves in like." This means that for one material to mix up completely with another, the two materials must be made up of the same kind of **molecules.** Oil and water are made up of different kinds of molecules, and so they don't mix together. In the second part of the experiment, the water in the bowl started to move back and forth and began to spill over the side back into the bathwater. This is because the bowl's sides aren't big enough to contain the wave.  Once the water starts moving it has to keep on moving until it hits something, such as the side of the bottle, or slops over the edge.

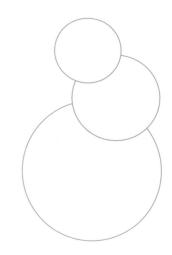

Water Glue

We think of certain things as sticky—chewing gum, some kinds of candy. And when you get something sticky on your skin, you often use water to get the sticky stuff off. But here's a weird fact about water—it's sticky, too! And if you think that's weird, listen to this! You may think of water as see-through, but it really has a "skin." Get ready to see why these things are true.

WHAT YOU NEED

- pennies
- salt
- tablespoon
- 2 plastic glasses (clear)
- water

WHAT YOU DO

1. Fill one glass with water and place the second glass on a flat, stable surface. Pour water from the first glass into the second until the second glass is filled to the very top.

2. Add one penny at a time to the glass of water by sliding the penny over the edge of the glass. Do not drop the penny into the water. How many pennies do you think you can put into the glass before the water spills over the edge?

3. Keep adding pennies one at a time. Each time you add a penny, look at the glass from the side. What does the water's surface look like when you look at it from this angle?

4. When the water begins to run down the outside of the glass, stop adding pennies. Dump out all the water and count the pennies. How many are in the glass?

5. Repeat step 1, only this time add a tablespoon (15 ml) of salt to the water in the first glass before you pour it into

the second. How many pennies did you add before the water began to drip?

WHAT HAPPENED?

When you added the first few pennies, the water did not slop over the edge of the glass. Instead, the water formed a shallow dome shape above the rim of the glass. This is because the molecules that water is made up of are attracted to each other more than they are attracted to the molecules that make up the air or the plastic glass. The parts that make up the top surface of the water form a **film** or "skin." This thin film, or skin, lifts up to form a dome shape as each additional penny is added and the pennies "stick" to the water. When enough pennies are added, the film cannot hold all the water beneath, so it breaks and the water begins to drip down the side of the glass. When salt is added to the water, it makes the water less sticky. This means that fewer pennies can be added before the water drips over.

Leaks Like a Sieve

*Do you like to cook? If so, you may have helped your mom or dad or a friend make spaghetti. If you did, you may have used something called a sieve. A **sieve** is a bowl-shaped piece of plastic or metal that is full of tiny holes. The holes allow the liquid to pass though, but catch any larger foods. (Sometimes, if a person cries easily, someone might say they "leak like a sieve" because so much water gushes from their eyes!) But, do sieves always work? This experiment will show you, and also teach you more about the things you learned in the last experiment. Let's see.*

WHAT YOU NEED

- bathtub
- paper tissue
- plastic bowl (with wide mouth)
- plastic fruit basket
- rubber band
- water
- wire mesh (thin, enough to cover the top of the bowl)
- adult helper

WHAT YOU DO

1. Fill the bowl to the top with water. Have your adult helper place the wire mesh over the top of the bottle and pull down on the mesh. Have him or her wrap an elastic band around the mesh to hold it in place so that no rough edges stick out.

2. Gently place your hand over the top of the mesh and quickly turn the bowl upside down. Take your hand away. Does the water pour out? Take a close look at the opening of the bottle while it is upside down. What do you see?

3. Let's try this again, this time with something with wider holes. Float a plastic fruit basket in the bathwater. It will stay on top of the water, if you place it there gently.

4. Take a small piece of paper tissue and lay it inside the basket. Is your basket still floating?

WHAT HAPPENED?

The water didn't go through the holes in the wire mesh or the fruit basket. That's because the molecules that make up water stick together on the surface of the water and form a thin film. When you look at the holes you can see the water bulging through, but it doesn't leak out. When you placed the tissue into the basket, the tissue **absorbed** some of the water and broke the film. The water then entered the basket and the basket sank.

Magnetic Magic

Sugar and soap—they don't sound like any-thing a magician would have up his or her sleeve, but you can use them to do an experiment that will make your family and friends think you know some hocus-pocus and teach you something interesting about science. In just a minute, you'll turn a straw and a toothpick into magic wands. Abracadabra! Here's how to make these simple items do your bidding.

WHAT YOU NEED

- ○ adult helper
- ○ bar of soap
- ○ granulated sugar (a small handful)
- ○ plastic drinking straw
- ○ plastic bowl (small)
- ○ tray
- ○ 2 wooden tooth-picks
- ○ water

WHAT YOU DO

1. Start preparing your magic wand by wetting a drinking straw at both ends. Dip one end in a little sugar. Then carefully turn the straw over and scrape the other end along a bar of soap.

2. Position the bowl on the tray, then place the two wooden toothpicks in the bowl so they float on top of the water. Make sure there is a little room between the tooth-

picks. Dip the sugared end of the magic wand in the water between the two toothpicks and say, "Come here, toothpicks!" What happens?

3. Next, turn the straw over and place the soapy end of the straw in the water between the toothpicks. Now, in your best magician voice, say, "Go away, toothpicks!" What happens now?

WHAT HAPPENED?

When you placed the sugared end of the straw between the two toothpicks, they moved towards the straw. This is because the sugar absorbed a small amount of the water. It only

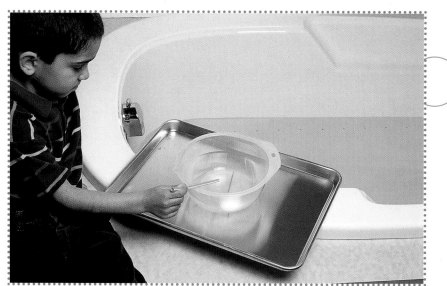

absorbed a little bit, but it was enough to cause the sticks to move. When you placed the end of the straw with the soap in between the two toothpicks, they moved apart. This is because the molecules of the water that make up its surface are attracted to each other—they move close to each other

and make a thin film-like skin on the water's surface. The soap broke apart the skin in the area between the two sticks, and the water moved away from the soap. As the water moved outward, it carried the sticks and they moved apart.

Water Tears

When raindrops fall from the sky in a cartoon, they look like teardrops. But do raindrops look like teardrops in real life? You might be surprised. Here's a way of studying water drops without having to put on your raincoat. In fact, you can stay warm and dry inside your own house or classroom. Get ready to see that maybe the sky isn't "crying" whenever there's a rainstorm after all!

WHAT YOU NEED

- adult helper
- bathtub
- eyedropper
- plastic bowl
- plastic cup
- tray
- turkey baster
- water

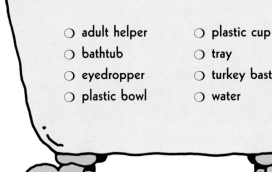

WHAT YOU DO

1. Have your adult helper fill the bowl with water until it is filled to the top. Place the bowl on the tray.

2. Fill the eyedropper with water. Hold the dropper straight up and down over the

surface of the water in the bowl, so that the end pointing down is about even with the level of your eyes. Slowly squeeze a drop of water from the dropper into the bowl. Can you see the drop of water as it leaves the end of the eyedropper? What shape is it?

3. Now turn the eyedropper sideways and squeeze out a drop. What shape is this drop? Try changing the angle of the eyedropper and see how this changes the shapes of the drops.

4. Repeat steps 1 through 3, this time using a turkey baster instead of an eyedropper. What shape are the water drops?

5. Next, have your adult helper hold the turkey baster higher above the surface of the water and squeeze a drop of water into the bowl. Watch what happens to the surface of the water as the drop lands on it.

6. Dip the plastic cup into the water in the bowl so that it's filled partway. Let the water in the bowl settle,  then hold the cup tilted over the bowl and let some of the water in the cup drip onto the water in the bowl. Watch the shape and size of the drops of water that fall from the cup. Are these drops larger or smaller than the ones that fell from the eye-dropper or turkey baster?

7. Have your adult helper turn on the faucet just a tiny bit so that drops of water fall from it. Have him or her adjust the faucet very slowly so that the drops fall faster and get larger. How large do the drops get before the water turns into a steady stream?

WHAT HAPPENED?

You made all sorts of water drops! Some of them were teensy-weensy, some small, some a little bigger, and some quite large. The sizes and shapes of the drops depend on a few things. You've probably already figured out that the drops are different sizes when the openings they drop through are different sizes. The eyedropper made tiny drops; the turkey baster made bigger drops, and the faucet made really big drops! Also, the water breaks apart into smaller drops if it falls a greater distance. And the flatter the surface the drop forms on, the larger the drop will be. One thing that affects the shapes of the drops is the film or skin that forms on the water's surface when the molecules that make up water move close together, which you learned about in "Water Glue" (see p. 27) and some other experiments.  No matter what size the drops are, if they drop onto this film, they are perfectly round, like a ball. Drops that are tear-shaped are that way because of the way the air around them affects them.

Knotty Water

It's hard to imagine that anyone other than a superhero or super-heroine can tie water in a knot. Do you think you can? Scoop up some water in your hand and try to change its shape. It can't be done, or can it? It might not seem like it just yet, but you're about to find out that you, too, have some super powers! With a little help from your mom, dad, brother, sister, or other favorite superhero, you can make a bunch of different streams of water all twist up into one stream of water. Here you go!

WHAT YOU NEED

- adult helper
- bathtub
- can opener
- duct or electrical tape
- hammer
- nail
- tin can (large)

WHAT YOU DO

1. Have your adult helper use a can opener to remove the top of the tin can. He or she must make sure there are no rough edges and wrap the can with duct tape to assure that no one's hands will get scratched.

2. Have your adult helper use the hammer and nail to poke four or five holes approximately 1 inch (2.5 cm) from the bottom of the can. The holes should be spaced ½ inch (1.3 cm) from each other.

3. Have your adult helper fill the can with water, and hold the water-filled can over the tub with the spouting holes facing toward you.

4. There should be several thin, separate streams of water spouting toward you. Use your fingers to pinch or join the streams of water together. Now there's only one stream of water!

5. Keeping your fingers near the holes in the can, put your fingers between the streams again. Now what happens to the stream of water?

WHAT HAPPENED?

When the water first came out of the holes, it ran in a separate stream  from each hole. When you gathered the water with your fingers, you held the streams together and they made one larger, single stream.

You broke the single stream when you placed your fingers between the holes, and they ran in individual streams again.

Lil' Hydroplane

There are special boats called hydroplanes. These boats move like high-powered race cars on the water, sometimes reaching speeds of over 300 miles (480 km) per hour! The jet engines on these boats release hot gases that make the boat move forward, and are so loud you can hear the roar of hydroplanes miles away from a race. Unless you're Godzilla, we bet your bathtub is too small to put a hydroplane in ... but you can create a tiny foil boat that works the same way.

WHAT YOU NEED

- adult helper
- bowl
- dishwashing liquid
- pencil
- scissors
- thimble
- toothpick
- tracing paper
- 2-inch (5-cm) square piece of aluminum foil
- water

WHAT YOU DO

1. Use the pencil to draw a small, simple house shape with a small, oblong "door" shape in the center of the front of the piece of aluminum foil (see photo following page). With scissors, cut along the outline of the house, cutting out the door shape. Discard the leftover foil. This is your miniature boat; the cutout door is the boat's "tank."

2. Fill the bowl (or bathtub) with water and place the boat in the water with its front end facing away from you.

3. Have your adult helper fill the thimble with dishwashing liquid. This is your "fuel." Dip one end of the toothpick into your fuel and place a drop of the fuel into the "tank."

WHAT HAPPENED?

Your boat jetted across the water! When the soap was placed into the "tank," the molecules that make up soap and the molecules that make up water spread out on the surface of the water, and they had only one direction they could move in. They moved out through the gap at the back of the boat. Just like the jet engines that move real **hydroplanes** by shooting out hot gases, the water shooting out the back of your boat drove it forward. The boat won't  keep working forever. Eventually, the surface of the water gets too full of dish soap and your boat stops moving. But fill the bowl or tub with fresh water and it will work again as good as new!

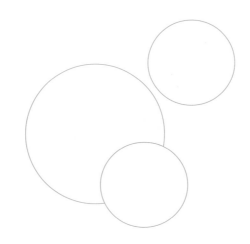

Holey Can!

*There is an old folktale about a brave little Dutch boy who lived in Holland. Holland has canals filled with water that is contained by dikes, or thick walls. When a **dike** sprang a leak, the little boy put his finger in the hole to prevent the water from flooding the lands. We don't know if that story's true, but this activity will give you some idea of what he must have been up against.*

WHAT YOU NEED

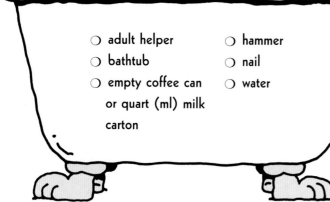

- ◯ adult helper
- ◯ bathtub
- ◯ empty coffee can or quart (ml) milk carton
- ◯ hammer
- ◯ nail
- ◯ water

the holes. How far do you think each of the streams of water would shoot out from the container? Would the water flow at the same speed from all three holes? Ask your adult helper what he or she thinks would happen.

WHAT YOU DO

1. Have an adult use the hammer and nail to poke three holes in the side of the can or carton. (If you're using a cardboard milk carton, he or she won't need the hammer.) The holes should be placed approximately 1 inch, 3 inches, and 6 inches, in a vertical line, from the bottom of the container.

2. Imagine the container were filled with water, so that water spouted out of each of

3. Now put your guesses to the test. Fill the tub with water and scoop water into the container. As you hold the filled container over the tub, watch the streams of water spouting from the holes. Did you guess correctly which way the streams would spout?

WHAT HAPPENED?

The spout of water pouring from the hole at the top stayed the closest to the container. The water from the middle hole poured out faster and farther than the top hole. The water poured out fastest and farthest from the bottom hole. This is because the water shooting out of the top hole has the least amount of water pressing down on it from above. The water coming from the second hole has a slightly greater amount of water pressing down on it. The water coming from the bottom hole has the greatest weight of water pushing it down and out, so it travels farthest and fastest. The weight of the water push-

ing down or outwards in a container is called the **water pressure.** The greater the water pressure, the further the stream of water will travel.

Water Cannon

In cities in the summer, sometimes people cool down in the water that shoots out from a fire hydrant. In other places, when the weather's hot, people cool off in their backyards by running through the cold water that shoots out from a sprinkler or a garden hose. How about making your own "water cannon" that works in the tub? Even if it's winter and you don't need to get cool, this is an experiment that's really fun.

WHAT YOU NEED

- adult helper
- bathtub
- balloon (approximately 14 to16 inches long)
- piece of duct tape
- about 2 × 3 inches (5 × 7.5 cm)
- hot-glue gun
- plastic pop bottle (large)
- water

WHAT YOU DO

1. Have your adult helper use the hot-glue gun to make a small hole in the side of the bottle approximately 1 inch (2.5 cm) from the bottom.

2. Fit the open end of the balloon over the mouth of the bottle so that the bottle's opening is completely covered and the balloon is securely attached to the bottle. Use your fingers to gently push the rest of the balloon down inside the bottle.

3. Use a small piece of duct tape to cover the hole in the side of the bottle.

4. Try to blow up the balloon with the duct tape covering the hole. What happens?

5. Peel back a section of the duct tape, so you can see the hole. Blow up the balloon, then quickly seal the hole with the duct tape. The balloon should stay inflated.

6. Fill the opening of the balloon with water. Aim the balloon at the side of the bathtub or wall (not into the bathroom, or toward the floor), then peel back the duct tape. Watch out!

7. Try this cannon outdoors on a warm day. You can show your friends this cool way to cool down!

WHAT HAPPENED?

You couldn't blow up the balloon when the hole was covered with duct tape because there was too much air inside the bottle. When you peeled the duct tape back and uncovered the hole, you could blow up the balloon. This is because the air could leave the bottle through the hole as you blew up the balloon. As  soon as you covered the hole, the balloon stayed inflated. This is because the air inside the balloon kept it inflated and the bottle kept the air outside from pressing in. When the duct tape was removed from the bottle, the water inside the balloon blew out of the bottle at a great speed. The water stretched the elastic balloon and it snapped back, letting the water out—fast!

On the Level

When your parents run a bath for you and then turn off the faucet, you expect the water to stay at the same level in the tub until you get in and splash around in it, right? The water doesn't move around and leave the tub, does it? No! But is it possible for the level of water to change without a kid splashing around in it? If you said "no," would you like to place a bet?

WHAT YOU NEED

- adult helper
- bathtub
- measuring cup or plastic drinking cup
- plastic funnel
- plastic or rubber tubing (2 or 3 feet [60–90 cm], clear, and wide enough to hold the funnel's spout)
- water

WHAT YOU DO

1. Insert the spout of the funnel into one end of the plastic tubing.

2. Hold the funnel under the tap and have your adult helper use the measuring cup to pour some water into the funnel. Keep adding water until the tubing is about halfway full.

3. Take the funnel out of the tubing. Hold the tubing so the ends of the tubing are at the same height. What are the water levels like at the different ends of the tubing?

4. Change the water levels inside the tubing by lifting or lowering one hand. What happens to the water levels as you do this?

WHAT HAPPENED?

Weird! The water stayed at the same level in the tubing, right? Even when you held one end of the tubing higher or lower than the other, the water levels in both ends of the tubing stayed the same. (Although if you had one end of the tubing really high, the water might have poured out of the other end!)

Not on the Level

In "On the Level," you saw that water wanted to stay flat and would even move around the plastic tubing to remain at the same level. Does that always happen? Hmmmmmmm. If you thought the results of the last experiment were surprising, get ready to be surprised again!

WHAT YOU NEED

- ○ adult helper
- ○ plastic bowl
- ○ plastic cup (clear)
- ○ tray
- ○ water

WHAT YOU DO

1. Fill the bowl approximately halfway with water and set it on a flat, sturdy surface. (If your bathtub or sink has a counter surrounding it, this will work, or you can set a tray down to use as your work surface.)

2. Dip the cup into the bowl and completely fill it with water. Turn the cup upside down in the bowl.

3. Keeping the cup level, slowly lift the cup up through the water so that the rim of the cup is just beneath the water's surface. If you have trouble doing this, ask your adult helper to give you a hand.

4. Where is the water level in the cup compared to the water level in the bowl? Why didn't the water fall out of the cup?

WHAT HAPPENED?

The strangest thing happened. The water level in the cup was higher than the water level in the bowl. This is because when the cup was filled with water, all the air was pushed out of the cup. When you lifted the cup up, some of the water fell into the bowl, leaving behind a **vacuum** or empty space inside the cup. The air outside the bowl pushed down on the surface of the water in the bowl and this held up the water that was still inside the cup.

Going Up?

It's easy to imagine a liquid coming down through a hose or a straw or a tube, because that's the way things fall—down. But can you imagine water moving up through a tube without your doing something like blowing or using a pump to make it go up? It's kind of hard. The water can't just get in an elevator and press a button, can it? But water can move upward all by itself, and you're about to find out how.

WHAT YOU NEED

- adult helper
- bathtub
- bowl (large)
- plastic or rubber tubing (3 feet)
- tray
- water

WHAT YOU DO

1. Have your adult helper fill the bowl approximately ¾ full. Set the tray on the side of the tub and place the bowl on it.
2. Fill the bathtub with water and hold the plastic tubing underwater for a few seconds until it fills with water. Have your adult helper pinch both ends of the tubing to keep the water from pouring out.

3. Keeping both ends of the tubing pinched, place one of its ends in the water in the bowl and the other end in the water in the tub. Un-pinch the ends of the tubing, but make sure one end remains underwater in the bowl and the other end stays over the water in the tub. (Otherwise you'll have a little flood!) What happens to the water in the bowl?

WHAT HAPPENED?

The water did something you didn't expect it to do, right? It rose up the tubing from the bowl and spurted water into the tub. In fact, you created a siphon. A siphon is a kind of tube used to move liquid from one place to another. As long as the tube is completely filled with the liquid—in this case, 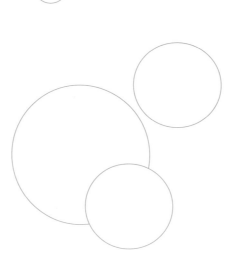 water—the liquid will travel upward in a siphon. The important thing is that the water always travels toward a lower point—in this case, the bathtub (and hopefully not the floor!).

Say It, Don't Spray It!

Straws make great science toys. Let's start with how a straw works: you put the straw into a yummy liquid, and as you suck through the straw, the drink moves up through the tube. Air pushes down on the surfaces of the liquid inside and outside of the straw. When you suck you reduce the air pressure inside the straw, but the outside pressure stays the same, so the liquid moves upward inside the straw.

WHAT YOU NEED

- bathtub
- plastic cup (tall)
- 2 drinking straws (wide)
- tray
- water

WHAT YOU DO

1. Fill the plastic drinking cup approximately ¾ full with water. Set the tray on the edge of the bath so that it is stable and put the cup on it.
2. Hold one straw straight up and down in the glass. The straw should be slightly taller than the glass.
3. Place the second straw at a right angle to the first straw, so the edges of the straws are just touching.

4. Point the second straw toward the wall behind the tub. Blow as hard as you can into the second straw and watch what happens to the first straw.

WHAT HAPPENED?

Usually, water doesn't come up a straw because air presses down through the straw onto the water. This pressing down is called **air pressure**. But when you blew into the second straw, you moved some air over the first straw. This lowered the air pressure inside the first straw slightly, and allowed water to come up the first straw. This water was blown into the opening of the second straw and when it met with your breath, it got pushed out and went flying against the side of your tub.

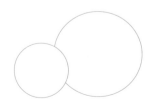

Diving Bell

Over three hundred years ago, a British scientist named Edmund Halley invented something called a *"diving bell."* Do you think it was a musical bell with flippers and a bathing cap and goggles? Of course not! It was a machine for going underwater that looked just like a bell. It was big enough to hold three people and could be lowered into parts of the ocean where it was too deep for people to dive safely. Here's how you can make your own diving bell for the bathtub.

WHAT YOU NEED

- adult helper
- bathtub
- pieces of tissue
- plastic cup (clear)
- plastic figurine (small)
- water

WHAT YOU DO

1. Place the figurine in the bottom of the plastic cup. Crumple up the pieces of paper tissue into a ball, and stuff it into the top of the cup.

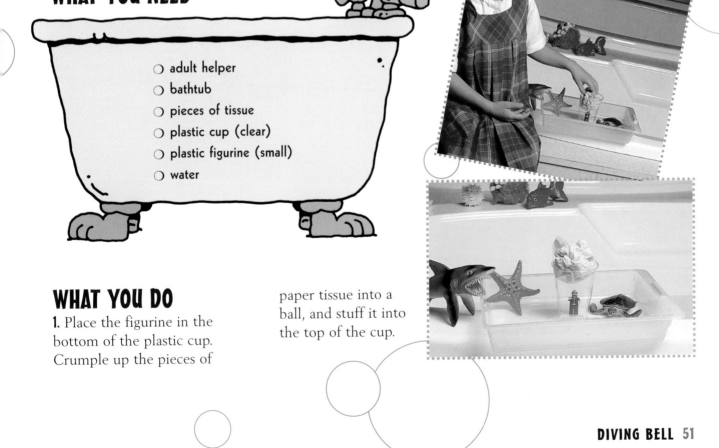

2. Fill the bathtub with water and turn the cup upside down over the water.

3. Slowly lower the open end of the cup into the water. Make sure you keep the cup level and do not tip it, or the water will fill the cup. Keep lowering the cup or have your adult helper lower the cup until it touches the bottom of the bathtub.

4. Keeping the cup level, lift it up and out of the water. Is your little diver dry or wet? How about the tissue?

WHAT HAPPENED?

The glass didn't fill with water because it was already filled with air. You can't see the air, but as you lowered the cup into the water, the air took up space that water would normally rush into. As you pushed the glass deeper into the water, some of the water pushed the air back farther into the cup because the deeper something is underwater, the more the water outside it presses in on it.

Burping Bottle

In some countries, when you're a guest for dinner at someone's house, it's polite to burp after dinner. True! It's considered the nicest way to say that you enjoyed the food. In other countries, burping at the dinner table is considered to be about the rudest thing you can do! If you have a little baby brother or sister, cousin or friend, you know that babies get forgiven for burping after they drink from their bottles. You'd better not try it, though, right? You just might get sent to your room and miss dessert! But here's a way to burp that won't get you in any trouble and will teach you something fun, too.

WHAT YOU NEED

- adult helper
- food coloring
- hammer
- modeling clay
- nail
- plastic cup
- plastic pen (disposable, clear)
- scissors
- three 16-ounce (500-ml) plastic pop bottles (with plastic caps)
- water

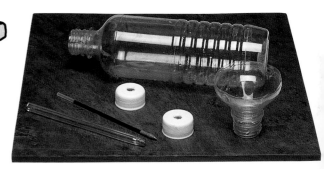

WHAT YOU DO

1. Have your adult helper cut one of the plastic bottles in half. This will be your funnel.
2. Have your adult helper use a hammer and nail to poke a hole in the middle of each of the plastic bottle caps. Each

hole should be wide enough to fit around one end of the disposable pen.

3. Have your adult helper remove the plastic ink cartridge from the pen. (This can be discarded, or set aside if the adult helper feels like putting the pen back together again later!) You will now have an empty plastic tube.

4. Gently push the plastic tube through one of the bottle caps so that a little bit of it extends past the screw-on end, with the screw-on end facing outward. Use your fingers and a little modeling clay to make a tight seal at the area where the pen and cap join. Do the same thing with the other cap to the opposite side of the tube.

5. Fill one of the two remaining pop bottles approximately halfway with water, and add a few drops of food coloring to make it a nice, bright color. Screw one cap onto the empty bottle and the other cap onto the bottle filled with colored water.

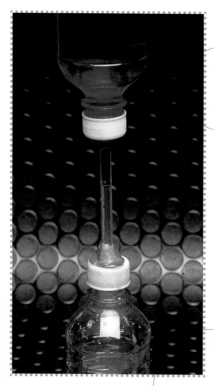

6. In one motion, turn the bottles upside down so that the full bottle is on top. Hold the full bottle straight without moving it from side to side. Watch what happened, then instead of holding the bottle straight, swirl it so the water inside begins to spin. Watch what happens to the water this time.

7. When the water is all in the bottom bottle, have your adult helper help you put your burping bottle together. Unscrew the cap from the empty bottle and screw the funnel onto the cap.

8. Use a cup to fill the top of the funnel with water. Give the bottle a little squeeze and watch what happens.

WHAT HAPPENED?

When you tried to empty the pop bottle by turning it straight upside down the water came out in gulps. First some  water comes out, then it slows and some air enters to replace the water, then more water comes out. When you swirled the water in the bottle as you turned it over, the water came out in a continuous stream. This is because the air could enter at the same time as the water was leaving. When you made the burping bottle the hole for water to leave through and air to enter through was much smaller. The burping bottle burped as the water left and the air entered in gulps.

Water Time

You may have noticed that your parents never forget to tell you when it's time to take a bath. So if their part of the job is to tell you when to get in, why not make your part of the job keeping tracking of how long you've been in there? (It will keep you from wrinkling up and looking like a prune, too!) You might already own a waterproof watch that you could take in, but here's a very unusual way you can time your bath that's more fun than just looking at your watch.

WHAT YOU NEED

- bathtub
- double-sided tape
- pen
- plastic measuring cup
- ruler
- 2 Styrofoam cups
- watch with a second hand
- water
- wooden skewer

WHAT YOU DO

1. Turn one of the cups upside down and have your adult helper use the wooden skewer to poke a hole in the middle of the cup's bottom.

2. Attach a long piece of double-sided tape vertically to one side of each of the cups. Lay the ruler on a flat surface and attach the cup with a hole right side up at the top of the ruler, and the second cup in the same way at the bottom of the ruler. Press down gently but firmly on the fronts of the cups to make sure they are securely in place. This is your "clock." Place another piece of double-sided tape from top to bottom along the back of the ruler, and attach this to the wall of your bathtub.

3. Fill the measuring cup with ½ cup (125 ml) of water. Pour the water in the hole. Use a watch to time the water dripping from the hole. After every minute, put your finger over the hole, and use a pen to mark the side of the cup with a line. How long does it take for all the water to drip from the top cup to the bottom cup?

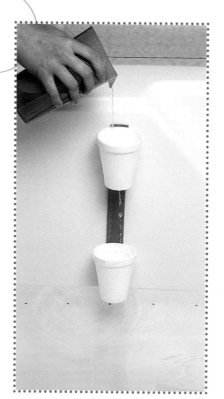

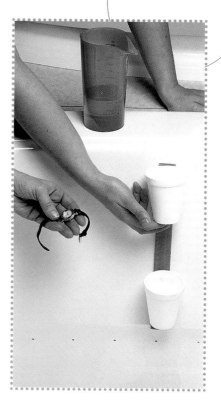

WHAT HAPPENED?

You made your own "water clock." It isn't the most accurate clock ever invented, but it does work for short periods of time. The water drips out of the hole at a regular speed for two reasons: because the hole stays the same size, and because the small amount of water in the cup means that there's not much water pres-sure, so the water drips slowly and evenly. In ancient China, people used clocks that worked like this to measure time. Of course they didn't use styro-foam cups to make their clocks, because Styrofoam hadn't been invented yet!

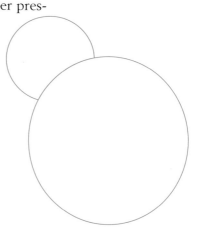

Rainbow Changes

Water comes in different colors: the water that comes out of your tap is a different color than the color of the ocean, and the color of the water in the ocean is different than the color of the water in a lake, right? The reason the waters are different colors is because of the different parts of the earth they come from and the things that are added to them. This experiment is more about fun than science, but it will show you how colors change the color of water and each other when they are combined. You're about to be an artist!

WHAT YOU NEED

- ○ adult helper
- ○ bathtub
- ○ food coloring
- ○ measuring cup
- ○ plastic cups (clear)
- ○ water

WHAT YOU DO

1. Fill four plastic cups with water. Have your adult helper help you add a drop or two of red food coloring to the water in one cup, a drop or two of blue to another cup, a drop or two of green to another cup, and a drop or two of yellow to another cup.

2. Pour a little of the red water into the yellow water. What color does it make?

3. Try adding a little blue water to the yellow water. What color does this make? One by one, try adding all of your different-colored waters to one another. How many different colors can you make?

WHAT HAPPENED?

Surprise! You created new colors when you combined the different colors. Red, blue, and yellow are called **primary colors** because they are not mixtures of other colors. But when you mixed one primary color with another one, they made new colors. The red and yellow made orange. The blue and yellow made green. The red and blue made purple. And the green and red made—well, kind of a yucchy brownish color, huh? The green, orange, and purple are called **secondary colors.**

Wheely Fun

When we stand on the Earth it feels perfectly still, but really it's turning around and around in space—sort of like a very slow wheel. This experiment isn't about the Earth, but it has a whole lot to do with going round and round.

WHAT YOU NEED

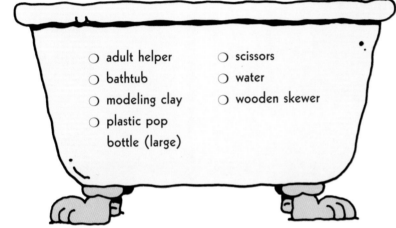

- ○ adult helper
- ○ bathtub
- ○ modeling clay
- ○ plastic pop bottle (large)
- ○ scissors
- ○ water
- ○ wooden skewer

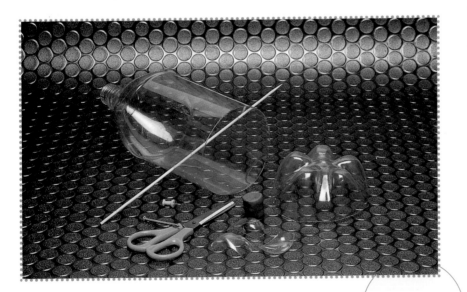

WHAT YOU DO

1. Have your adult helper cut the end off a pop bottle, approximately 2 inches (5 cm) from the bottom. Don't throw this away.

2. Have your adult helper cut two holes on opposite sides of the plastic bottle, approximately halfway from the mouth to the cut end of the bottle. Next, he or she can thread the wooden skewer through the hole on one side of the bottle, through the open space inside the bottle, and out the hole on the other side. The amounts of skewer showing on either side of the bottle should be about the same.

3. Have your adult helper use scissors and the leftover, curved part of the plastic bottle that you saved in step 1 to cut four strips of plastic, about 1 to 2 inches (2.5 to 5 cm) long. By cutting along the curves of the bottle's bottom and sides, he or she can create little curved plastic shapes that will act like spokes in a wheel.

4. Now it's your turn. Take a piece of the modeling clay and use your hands to mold it around the skewer inside the bottle so that it makes an even sausage shape around the skewer, about in the middle of the skewer.

5. Have your adult helper insert the four pieces of curved plastic into the skewered piece of clay. One of the short ends of each of the plastic pieces should be pushed into the clay just a little bit, and all the pieces should be positioned so that they are parallel to one another. This is your "wheel."

6. Have your helper hold the wheel under a running faucet in the tub, and watch it go!

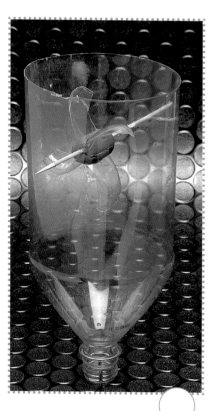

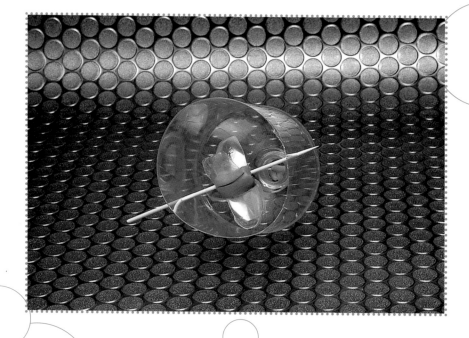

WHAT HAPPENED?

You made a water wheel! When the water hits the spokes, it causes them to move. As each spoke moves, the next one is hit by the stream of water, and the wheel spins. Water wheels are used to turn the movement of water into **energy** that can be used for all kinds of things. Water wheels are used to make machinery work, even to turn little machines that make **electricity**—although as you know, you should never, never use water and electricity in the same place. Your water wheel is too small to use for machinery, but just the right size to have some fun!

Water Garden

*When seasons change and it's time for flowers to bloom, they sometimes open very quickly. One kind of flower, called a **hibiscus,** opens and closes in the same day! Others, such as roses, can take weeks and weeks to grow and bloom. You probably haven't got the time to sit and watch a flower's bud open, but watch how you can make another kind of flower bloom in a bowl of water.*

WHAT YOU NEED

- ○ adult helper
- ○ colored paper (a few different colors)
- ○ plastic bowl
- ○ scissors
- ○ water

WHAT YOU DO

1. Use the scissors to cut (or have your adult helper cut) a few small squares of paper in different colors. Fold the four corners of each square over evenly, so that you have a slightly smaller square.

2. Fill the bowl with water and gently place your small, colored squares on the water's surface, with the folded parts up. Now just sit back and watch for a few minutes...

WHAT HAPPENED?

As the water moved into the paper, your little squares bloomed like flowers in the water. The paper has small spaces that the water can move into and as the water moves, it pulls more water along. The paper becomes less stiff when it is wet, so the corners opened up like petals. Flower blooms also open up because of the movement of liquids in the plant, just like the water in your paper flowers.

Isn't That Swell?

When you sit in a bath for a long time, something strange happens to your skin. The tips of your fingers and the bottom of your toes are all puckered up. That seems pretty weird because you'd think that spending all that time in a bath would make you puff up. What's happening?

WHAT YOU NEED

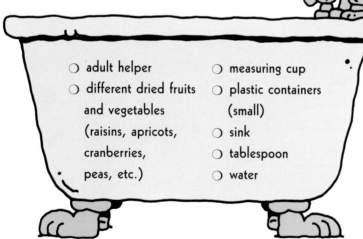

- ○ adult helper
- ○ different dried fruits and vegetables (raisins, apricots, cranberries, peas, etc.)
- ○ measuring cup
- ○ plastic containers (small)
- ○ sink
- ○ tablespoon
- ○ water

WHAT YOU DO

1. Place one tablespoon (15 ml) of each of the dried items in a separate container.

2. Add ¼ cup (60 ml) of warm water to the fruits or vegetables in each container.

3. Place the containers on a flat, stable surface.

4. Fill the sink with warm water and put your hand in the water for ten or so minutes.

5. Take your hand out of the water and see if you have wrinkles on your fingers. Compare your wrinkled skin to the shape of the dried materials in their containers. Do you notice anything funny? What happened to the dried foods when they were left in liquid?

WHAT HAPPENED?

The dried fruits became less wrinkled when they sat in the warm water, but you became more wrinkled! That seems weird, but it makes perfect sense. Both of these things

happened for the same reason; the water moved across an invisible "wall" into another area that has more dissolved materials in it. In the case of the fruits and you, the wall is built out of the cells that make up your skin. Sugars and salts and other materials are inside you and the fruit on the other side of the wall. The water moves into the fruit to plump it up. The water also moves into your skin to plump it up. Your skin is made up of different layers, and the parts of your body underneath the top layer don't get plumped up, so your skin wrinkles because it is stretched.

Don't worry though, your skin will shrink back when it dries out, and the wrinkles will be all gone!

Smooth Water

At the sink or a bathtub, scoop some water in your hands. Does it feel "hard" or "soft"? Now, wrap an ice cube in a towel, and hold it in your hands. Does it feel "hard" or " soft"?

You probably said that the ice cube was hard and the water was soft, right? But sometimes we use other meanings for the words "hard" and "soft" when we talk about water. Let's see if you can tell the difference between water that is hard and water that is soft.

WHAT YOU NEED

- ○ dishwashing liquid
- ○ Epsom salts
- ○ felt marker
- ○ jar (large)
- ○ masking tape
- ○ rainwater or snow
- ○ teaspoon
- ○ 3 plastic containers (small, clear, all the same size, with lids)
- ○ water (from the tap)

WHAT YOU DO

1. Collect some rainwater in a large jar. If it's not raining, or if it's winter (or you live in a place where it snows a lot), you can also use freshly fallen snow. If you do use snow, make sure you only use snow that is not directly touching the ground and is completely white.

2. Put 1 cup (250 ml) of rainwater or melted snow in one of the containers. Put a small piece of masking tape on the side of the container and write the number "1" on the tape.

3. Place 1 cup (250 ml) of rainwater or melted snow in another container. Add ½ teaspoon (2 ml) of **Epsom salts** to the water. Put a small piece of masking tape on the side of the container and write the number "2" on the tape.

4. Place 1 cup (250 ml) of tap water into the third container. Put a small piece of masking tape on the side of the container and write the number "3" on the tape.

5. Add a teaspoon of dishwashing liquid to the liquid in each container and tightly screw the lids onto all the containers.

6. Shake each container for about a minute.

Which one has the most soap bubbles inside?

WHAT HAPPENED?

The container marked "1" has more bubbles than the container marked "2," while the container marked "3" has different amounts of bubbles depending on where you live. The reason that some containers have more bubbles than others is because the water in the containers is different. The rainwater is called "soft" water, because it doesn't contain any **minerals.** Minerals are special kinds of salts found in the earth. When rainwater soaks into the ground, it absorbs minerals in the soil and this changes the **soft water** into **hard water**. The minerals in the hard water mix with the soap to make a soap scum that doesn't form bubbles. Epsom salts are natural minerals found in the earth.

Pretty Pictures

Pretty pictures are often hung in frames on the wall. But have you ever heard of a picture on the bathtub wall? It sounds a little strange, but you can make pictures of just about anything you want to and clean your tub safely at the same time. (You can also try making them in a sink.) Get ready to paint away! And remember to clean up your pictures afterward. You can always make more later!

WHAT YOU NEED

- adult helper
- baby shampoo (⅓ cup [80 ml])
- bathtub, sink, or other suitable surface (see below)
- cornstarch (1 tablespoon)
- cotton swab or toothpicks
- food coloring
- paper cups (small)
- spoon
- shaving foam
- water

1. Have your adult helper make sure that your bathtub, sink, or other surface is safe to "paint" on. You're not using real paint, and the kind you are using can be wiped off most regular tile surfaces. But some natural, porous tiles, such as limestone, are not recommended as painting surfaces.

2. Get ready to make amazing pictures! In a paper cup, mix together ⅓ cup of baby shampoo and 1 tablespoon of cornstarch to make a paste. You can use the end of a cotton swab or your fingers.

3. Spoon or pour a little of some of the mixture you just made into a few different paper cups. Add two to three drops of a different color of food coloring to the mixture in each cup, and mix it well. We used red, blue, and green, but you can use other colors, or mix colors together to make new colors.

4. Use your fingers to paint beautiful pictures on the inside of your bathtub or sink, or other safe surface. We used a little bit of shaving foam to help make our funny face, but you can make all kinds of pictures just with your new paint.

WHAT HAPPENED?

When you added the corn-starch to the baby shampoo, the shampoo became a little thicker. This made your finger paint stick to the tub, sink, or other surface. The food coloring gives the paint its different colors so you have a rainbow of choices!

Sound Waves

Does your voice sound the same on land as it does underwater? If you were swimming underwater and someone called your name, what do you think you would you hear? Here's a simple experiment that will let you find out and have fun with a friend at the same time—and neither of you have to go in the water!

WHAT YOU NEED

- ○ adult helper
- ○ bathtub
- ○ a friend
- ○ plastic whistle or recorder
- ○ scissors
- ○ 2 Styrofoam cups
- ○ water

3. Have a friend put the end of the whistle of the recorder where sound comes out so that it is just barely in the water, then play a tune. What does it sound like when you hear it underwater?

WHAT YOU DO

1. Have your adult helper cut out the bottoms of the Styrofoam cups.

2. Fill the bathtub (or sink) with water. Place one cup over one of your ears. Tilt your head sideways and put the other end of the cup so that it just barely touches the water's surface. Put your hand over your other ear.

4. Try this again. This time, you do the same thing, but have your friend place the smaller end of the other Styrofoam cup just barely on the water's surface, then speak into the cup. How does his or her voice sound?

WHAT HAPPENED?

The whistle or recorder and your friend's voice sound quite different when you hear them through the water. Sound travels about four and a half times faster in water than it does in air. The sound made through the recorder or cup by your friend's breath or voice moved from the air into the water, then into the air around your ear before you heard it.

You're Getting Warmer...

A funny thing happens when you take a bath after you have been out in the cold. You get an adult to run the water and check the temperature to make sure it's not too hot. When it seems like it is just the right temperature—not too hot and not too cold—you jump in the bath to warm your cold body. But...yikes! For some reason, the bathwater feels too hot when you get in. Why is that? Here's a way to discover how water can feel different depending on the temperature of your skin.

WHAT YOU NEED

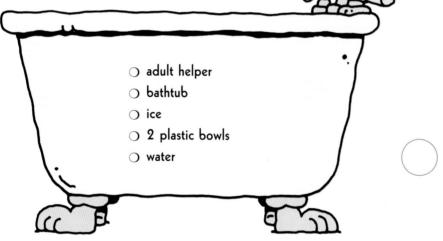

- ○ adult helper
- ○ bathtub
- ○ ice
- ○ 2 plastic bowls
- ○ water

WHAT YOU DO

1. Fill a small bowl with ice cubes. Add some water to the bowl.

2. Have your adult helper fill a bowl with really warm water, making very sure that the water is not too hot.

3. Have your adult helper run a bath for you. (The temperature of the bathwater should be cooler than the water in the bowl, but not too cool.)

4. Place one of your hands in the bowl of cold water for about ten seconds. Remove your hand and dunk it in the bathwater. How does it feel?

5. Place your other hand in the bowl of warm water for about ten seconds. Remove your hand, then dunk it in the bathwater. Now how does the bathwater feel?

WHAT HAPPENED?

When you put the hand that had been in the cold water into the bath, the bathwater felt like it was burning your hand. When you put the hand that had been in the bowl of very warm water into the bath, the bathwater felt  really cold. This is because your skin tells you that the water is hotter or colder, but not what the temperature is. When you cool down your skin, any increase in temperature feels hot. When you heat up your skin, any decrease in temperature feels cool. In the summer, when you are hot and jump into a swimming pool or dash through the sprinklers or into the ocean, the water seems to feel like ice for just this reason.

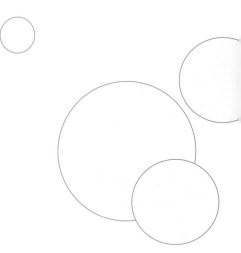

Where's the Money?

When a magician performs magic tricks, he or she sometimes talks about "creating illusions." An **illusion** is something that fools your mind into thinking it is seeing something else. Your eyes send mixed messages to your brain and your brain has to decide which message is correct. Do you think you can fool your brain? With this experiment, you can perform a magic trick on yourself and learn something new.

WHAT YOU NEED

- ○ adult helper
- ○ bathtub
- ○ coin
- ○ plastic bowl (large, clear)
- ○ plastic cup

WHAT YOU DO

1. Set the plastic bowl down on the edge of the bathtub. (If you don't have a bathtub, find a table or other flat surface that you can kneel beside so that your eyes are at about the same level as the surface.)

2. Put a coin in the center of the bowl.

3. Kneel down next to the bathtub and and peek over the side of the bowl so that you can just barely see the coin. Move your head slowly downward until you can't see the coin anymore. Stay right there. Don't move a muscle.

4. Have your adult helper slowly add water into the bowl until the coin "reappears."

WHAT HAPPENED?

When some water was poured into the bowl, you could see the coin again! You see the coin because the light in the room reflects, or bounces off of, the coin. Light travels at different speeds in different materials. When light goes between the air and the water, it is refracted, which means it bends. The bending of the light allows you to see the coin through the water when you couldn't see it through the air. Next time you go swimming, try looking down at your legs in the water and you will see that they look different under the water because of **refraction**.

Down Periscope

"Where's the Money?" (see p. 72), you learned that things sometimes look different when they are underwater. But do you think they look bigger or smaller when you look at them through water? There's an instrument called a periscope that uses mirrors and lenses to see things around corners and in other places where a straight view of something is blocked—even underwater! Here's a way to make your own periscope.

WHAT YOU NEED

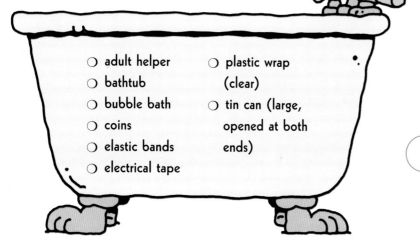

- adult helper
- bathtub
- bubble bath
- coins
- elastic bands
- electrical tape
- plastic wrap (clear)
- tin can (large, opened at both ends)

WHAT YOU DO

1. Have your adult helper wrap electrical tape around the bottom and top rims of the tin can. This will prevent you from cutting yourself on any rough or sharp edges.

2. Rip a piece of plastic wrap large enough to fit over the bottom of the tin can. Pull the plastic wrap tight and use an elastic band to hold it in place.

3. Have your adult helper run a thick bubble bath.

4. Drop several coins into the bath before you get in.

5. Place the wrapped end of the **periscope** into the water and look through the top end. Can you find the coins using this special tube? Do they seem to be bigger or smaller that when

they are out of the water? Or are they the same size?

WHAT HAPPENED?

Your periscope allowed you to see the coins in the bottom of the bath. The bubbles were lighter than water so they floated at the top. One end of the periscope was below the level of the bubbles so you could see right through them. The coins probably looked about the same size as you would expect, unless the plastic wrap was a little bit loose,

in which case they looked a little bit larger than expected. If the wrap was a little bit loose, the water came up into the tube a little bit and the light from the coins was bent or refracted.

This bending made the coins look bigger than they are.

The Perfect Solution!

Whether you have ever blown bubbles before or not, you are in for a big treat. It's easy to do and so much fun to watch big, round, shimmering bubbles float up, up, and away like balloons! What's especially cool is that with just a few simple ingredients from the kitchen, you get to make your own home-made bubble solution. It's easy and fun.

WHAT YOU NEED

○ adult helper
○ drinking straw
○ homemade bubble solution
○ measuring cup
○ plastic container (large, with lid)
○ plastic tray (flat) or cookie sheet to use as a bath tray
○ your hand
○ washcloth

WHAT YOU DO

1. Start by preparing the perfect bubble solution. Mix together the following: ¼ cup (80 ml) Joy ™, 3 cups (750 ml) water, and a tablespoon (15 ml) of glycerine or white corn syrup in a large plastic container with a lid. Place the lid on the jar and give it a good shake to mix up the ingredients.

2. Remove the lid and dip your hand into the solution, then join your fingers to form a circle. You should see a thin film of bubble solution. Blow with your breath through this film to create a bubble.

3. Next, try using a straw to blow into the solution to create mini-bubbles. (Be careful not to get bubble solution in your eyes. If you accidentally do this, wash your hands in the tub and use a clean, wet washcloth to soak your eyes.)

WHAT HAPPENED?

Your bubbles went—pop!—when they came in contact with a dry surface. As long as the bubbles touched something wet, like water in a bathtub, they didn't pop. And that's the end of the lesson ... since you've worked hard and learned all the fun facts about science in this book, we say... just grab those bubbles, and blow away!

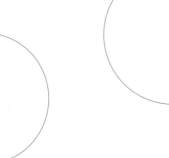

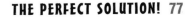

Glossary

absorb:to take in a substance, such as water.

air pressure:the force that air puts on things.

density:the amount of mass in an object per unit of volume.

dike:a thick wall or bank of earth used to prevent floods from a river or ocean.

diving bell:a device invented by Edmund Halley and used by divers to go to greater depths.

electricity:a flow of electric energy.

energy:anything that has the ability to cause things to move.

entropy:a measure of the amount of disorder, entropy naturally increases over time.

Epsom salts:a mineral found in nature; sometimes part of bath salts.

expand:to get bigger.

film:a thin layer of something such as water.

float:to stay on the surface, of water for example.

hard water:water containing minerals.

hibiscus:a type of flower.

hydroplane:a small, fast boat that skims the surface of the water.

illusion:when your eyes play tricks on you.

machine:a device used to make work easier.

mineral:a natural substance that makes up rocks.

molecules:tiny particles of materials such as water, soap, and air.

periscope:an instrument that uses lenses and mirrors to see things that are blocked from view.

water pressure:the force that water puts on things.

primary color:colors that are not mixtures of other colors—red, yellow and blue.

secondary color:colors made by mixing primary colors together—green, orange and purple.

sieve:a plastic or metal container with tiny holes in it.

siphon:a bent tube used for moving water from a higher container to a lower one.

soft water:water that is free of minerals.

temperature:a measure of how hot or cold something is.

thermometer:a device used to measure temperature.

refraction:the bending of light as it goes from one material into another material.

vacuum:empty space.

volume:the amount of space something takes up.absorb, 30, 32